The Wedding of Q and U

Written by Denise Dillon-Hreha
Illustrated by Sheri Mathews

AuthorHouse™
1663 Liberty Drive
Bloomington, IN 47403
www.authorhouse.com
Phone: 833-262-8899

Because of the dynamic nature of the Internet, any web addresses or links contained in this book may have changed since publication and may no longer be valid. The views expressed in this work are solely those of the author and do not necessarily reflect the views of the publisher, and the publisher hereby disclaims any responsibility for them.

This book is printed on acid-free paper.

ISBN: 978-1-4259-8040-5 (sc)

Library of Congress Control Number: 2006910960

Print information available on the last page.

Published by AuthorHouse 11/05/2020

authorHOUSE®

I dedicate this book to all of my students, both past and present, who have inspired me to teach the spelling rule of Qu in a creative way. I hope you all had fun at the wedding. You helped make teaching fun!

To my beautiful daughter, Chloe and my sweet son, Aidan – I look so forward to reading this book to both of you as you grow to be the smart, beautiful children you are. You are what life is all about. I love, love, love you.

To my wonderful, supportive husband, Michael – You have never let me stop reaching for the stars. Thank you for your tireless support. I love you.

To my mom and dad – You will always have my gratitude for helping me to become strong and achieve great things. Love always!

To Sheri, my friend – You are so talented and funny. I am honored to be on this journey with you. God speed.

To my talented friend, Randi – Whose music helped make our weddings seem real. The check is in the mail!

-DH

I dedicate this book to my entire loving and supportive family who is always there to give me their words of encouragement.

To my mother, who always has more faith in me during the times that I don't.

To both of my sisters, Tracey and Jamie, who are always proud of my achievements, no matter how big or small.

To my nephew Christian, and my niece Darian, for all of their creative ideas and and time spent coloring pages. I would never have gotten through this without you!

To Denise, my friend, who never ceases to pass an opportunity my way. We have shared countless memorable experiences that will forever keep me entertained. Thank you for all of them.

-SM

One warm, sunny day in Syllable City, the letter Q was walking along Alphabet Avenue with some other letter friends.

Quiz

Her letter friends joined together to make some words. They left Q out because the sound her letter made just did not fit into their words. She was sad.

Quart

Q did not like feeling sad and lonely, and she walked away feeling quite blue even though her friends tried to make her stop.

Queen

Just as she was walking home along Punctuation Place, Q had a brilliant idea that made her smile. She decided that she needed a lifetime partner. This partner would have to be someone who would never leave her feeling lonely. But who would it be?

Question Mark

Q thought and thought and thought.

Quiet

She dreamed and dreamed and dreamed.

Queasy

At last, Q figured out exactly which letter she would ask to be her partner! She was so excited.

Quartet

She was on her way to see the letter U, who lived in Vowel Valley.

$$4 \div 2 = ②$$

Quotient

You see, Q liked the other 24 letters of the alphabet, but the letter U was her favorite. So she asked U to be her partner.

Quintuplets

U was so flattered that Q asked if he would be her partner. They spent so much time together that they became inseparable. So wherever Q went, so did U.

Quill

The two letters decided to get married right away. That way, whenever Q was going to be the first letter in a word, U would follow along to make their words really quick.

Quench

Together their sound would be unique. Letters from Readers Road would remember how to read their words.

Quiver

Letters from Spellers Circle would remember how to spell their words.

Quaker

The day of the wedding, all the letters, spellers and readers were invited to the ceremony. It was a big celebration!

Quilt

The letter Q said her vows first.   She said...

I, the letter Q
Take you, the letter U
To be my letter partner
To stand beside me in every word
In cursive or in manuscript
One syllable or five
To never let another letter stand
between us.
I promise, to lead you in each word
So that all of our words may be
spelled correctly
For as long as the English language
shall exist.

Then the letter U said his vows. He promised...

I, the letter U
Take you, the letter Q
To be my letter partner
To stand beside me in every word
In cursive or in manuscript
One syllable or five
To never let another letter stand between us.
I promise, to follow you in each word
So that all of our words may be spelled correctly
For as long as the English language shall exist.

LIBERTY

Quarter

After saying their vows and exchanging rings, the mayor of Syllable City pronounced the letters official "Letter Partners."

Quicksand

From that day on, Q and U were to be at the beginning of many important words. That is why when you see a word that begins with Q, the letter U will be sure to follow!

Quadruplets

Quail

Quadruplets

Quaker

Quart

Quarter

Quarterback

Quartet

Quilt

Quintuplets

Quiver

Quiz

Quotation Marks

$$4 \div 2 = \boxed{2}$$

Quotient

About the Author

Denise Dillon-Hreha is a special education teacher in Howell, New Jersey. She has been an elementary school educator for the past twelve years. Denise has earned a Bachelor's Degree in Elementary Education/English in 1996 and a Master's Degree in Special Education in 2001 from Kean University. She is certified to become a school principal or supervisor. Denise is currently writing her dissertation to earn her doctoral degree from Seton Hall University in 2007. She has taught as an adjunct professor at the graduate level. Denise's two young children, Chloe and Aidan, have been an inspiration to many of her ideas. She has been reading to them since birth, hoping to share and instill her love of reading. The illustrator, Sheri Mathews, has been a friend for many, many years through high school and college.

About the Illustrator

Sheri Mathews is graphic artist ten years in the making. She has earned a Bachelor's Degree in the Graphic Arts in 1996 from Kean University, and has been working in the field ever since. This has been her first experience with illustrating and looks forward toward the continuing journey.

Printed in the United States
By Bookmasters